A
Beautiful
Prayer

Answering Common Misperceptions about Centering Prayer

Other Books by Peter Traben Haas

The God Who Is Here: A Contemplative Guide to Transforming Your Relationship with God and the Church

Centering Prayers: A One-Year Daily Companion for Going Deeper into the Love of God

A Living Lent: A Contemplative Daily Companion for Lent and Holy Week

My Yes Is Yours: A Contemplative Daily Companion for Advent and Christmas

About the Cover

"The image represents God as joined mind and heart, as the crown and roots. God's omniscience often is portrayed through the symbol of the eye. The eye is the window to the soul and spirit, the organ of spiritual perception. The Old Testament prophet Ezekiel described God's glory and His throne upon wheels within wheels full of eyes (Ezekiel 1:18,10:12). This drawing started when I saw eye-like figures in the branches of a tree. Then, inspired by a majestic oak that I had been looking at for months, I incorporated those eyes spontaneously, in place of the leaves. The root system is in balance with the crown, the Divine mind connected with the Divine Heart. The multiplicity of hands, perhaps signify the generosity of God - bestowing Love tens of thousands fold. The hands are symbolic of labor, creativity, and love. Interestingly, a viewer can turn the picture upside down and still perceive that unity and balance and harmony. The three birds represent the Holy Trinity, the Holy Spirit above all, and the two birds - the Father and the Son - represent the perfect Agape - Love of the Trinity, sustaining the Creation by the flowing in of the Holy Spirit and Where God is - I AM."

Tatiana Nikolova-Houston
SacredIllumination.com
Austin, TX

A
Beautiful
Prayer

Answering Common Misperceptions about Centering Prayer

~

Dr. Peter Traben Haas

Published by ContemplativeChristians.com
Austin, TX

A Beautiful Prayer:
Answering Common Misperceptions about Centering Prayer
© 2014 Peter Traben Haas
All rights reserved. Published 2014.
Second Printing, 2015.

Unless otherwise noted, Scripture references are taken from the New Revised Standard Version. All rights reserved.

Library of Congress Cataloging-in-Publication Data

Haas, Peter Traben (1972 –   )
A Beautiful Prayer: Answering Common Misperceptions about Centering Prayer / *Peter Traben Haas*
ISBN-13: 978-1499290677
ISBN-10: 1499290675
p.cm.
  1.   Spiritual life – Christianity. 2. Centering Prayer. I. Title.

BV 4501.3.H33 2014

20100

Printed in the United States of America

Dedicated to:

Spiritual Forerunners and Friends in the Silence –
Everywhere

&

Shannon
Everything

Contents

"Until we all reach unity in the faith and in the knowledge of the Son of God and become mature, attaining to the whole measure of the fullness of Christ."

— Ephesians 4.13

"These things God has revealed to us through the Spirit; for the Spirit searches everything, even the depths of God."

— I Corinthians 2.10

"Sometimes God speaks to us when we don't even know it is God. I think God has many ways of speaking to us...God speaks to our hearts and minds, and sometimes God's message has nothing to do with words. God is love and intelligence and life. More than anything we say God is, or even imagine God is. God is the one universal Presence and Power and is seeking to express Truth and beauty and good through all of us and for all of us."

— James Dillet Freeman

A
Beautiful
Prayer

Introduction:

A Personal Note to the Reader

While the contemplative disposition often prefers silence, sometimes it's useful to speak up. In this short book, after a brief description of the Centering Prayer method, I will respond to five frequent misperceptions about Centering Prayer. As a pastor, my aim was to write and share this resource in the spirit of love, which, I trust, surpasses all ideas and disagreements of perspective. Primarily, I wish for all who read this resource the utmost grace, goodness and growth in Christ. For that reason I close the book with an extended reflection on the definitions related to Centering Prayer, particularly focusing on the words *Contemplative* and *Unitive,* and three invitations and a personal prayer.

I'm starting with love because, as I have shared the method of Centering Prayer in churches and faith communities around the country, I have discovered that while there is sometimes fear and hostility toward the contemplative dimension of Christian experience, there are really just a few questions, concerns and resistances to Centering Prayer that keep coming up. When we can move through the questions using scripture and discernment, folks often release their objections not so much because they have been won over by powerful intellectual or doctrinal proofs, but because, in the silence and in the surrender, they often feel the warmth of God's love and the closeness of the living Christ, by the still power of the Holy Spirit. That's not to diminish the intellectual concerns people may have. No doubt, the concerns and questions are very core to folk's sense of faith and experience of the Christian life.

So, in the end even if people may disagree about the practice of Centering Prayer, or simply not see its relevance for their lives, I do hope all who read this resource and ponder its ideas will feel the love of God through these simple words offered here. Thus, this short book is an attempt to address these few but important friction points that might be preventing people from experiencing one of the most important, meaningful, and beautiful spiritual practices we can partake in during this unfolding journey we call a lifetime.

Every blessing growing deeper in Christ;
Going wider in God's love; Giving more of your "self" to the
Spirit; In the silence of surrender.

Peter Traben Haas
Autumnal Equinox, 2014

Description:

What is the Method of Centering Prayer?

The method of Centering Prayer, as taught by Father Thomas Keating and Contemplative Outreach, is very simple and follows a four-fold path:

1. *Choose a sacred word as the symbol of your intention to consent to God's presence and action within.*

2. *Sitting comfortably and with eyes closed, settle briefly and silently introduce the sacred word as the symbol of your consent to God's presence and action within.*

3. *When engaged with your thoughts, return ever so gently to your sacred word.*

4. *At the end of the prayer period, remain in silence with eyes closed for a couple of minutes.*

Let's take a deeper look at each of the guidelines of the method of Centering Prayer.

Guideline one:

Choose a sacred word as the symbol of your intention to consent to God's presence and action within.

The sacred word is sacred because you choose it and it represents your consent to deepen your experience of

God's presence and action within. The sacred word should be simple and short, usually not more than two syllables. This makes it easy to say. It should be simple, in that it shouldn't be a word that triggers too much emotional reaction. Good examples are: stillness, quiet, love, Abba, Adonai, Kyrie, peace, Jesus.

The sacred word isn't a mantra. We don't keep repeating the word over and over again throughout the duration of the prayer period.

The sacred word is a symbol. It's also a common meditation "tool" by which the spirit and mind consent to God as an act of intention. We are not focusing on the sacred word. We are not becoming more and more mindful of the sacred word. We just need a "mind tool" to help us with our thoughts by returning us to our intention to consent to God in the silence.

As the mind inevitably floods with thoughts, the sacred word gives us a simple gesture to help us return to the intention and purpose for our sitting in the silence.

Guideline two:

> *Sitting comfortably and with eyes closed, settle briefly and silently introduce the sacred word as the symbol of your consent to God's presence and action within.*

When we close our eyes it's as if half the world goes away. Closing our eyes is a simple gesture of our deepening consent to the interior, where we can experience the presence and action of the Holy Spirit. By closing our eyes, it's as if we are saying "Yes" to God. We are saying that we wish to commune more deeply and create an atmosphere in which our awareness gives its attention to that deepest part of our experience that we name "abiding in Christ."

We give our attention and our intention to resting in God, and discovering what it might mean for us to experience an increasing Pleroma (or fullness) of Participation in the divine nature, activating more completely the "mind of Christ" in us through our deepening surrender – what theologians call *kenosis*, literally meaning self-emptying (Philippians 2.1-14).

Sitting comfortably is important so that there are as few distractions and physical discomforts during the prayer period as possible, which is suggested to last at least 20 minutes. Just doing the prayer is challenging enough! No need to make it more challenging to you by sitting in a position that you are not comfortable in or that causes physical strain or pain.

We introduce the sacred word in our heart and mind. It's not said with the mouth or lips. It's an interior awareness, like drawing the mind to the heart by recalling a loved one's face, so to speak. It's a sensation more than a saying. We are simply using the word to help the mind move deeper into the place where we discover that we are more available and pliable to the presence and action of the Spirit of God.

For some, a sacred word is not useful or effective. In that case, following ones breath might be more meaningful, or for others, choosing an image to return to in the mind – something contemplative David Frenette calls the sacred glance, an inward glance within.

Guideline three:

> *When engaged with your thoughts, return ever so gently to your sacred word.*

In a sense, this is the only thing we actually do in the method of Centering Prayer. We return ever so gently to our sacred word. The word "thoughts" covers everything we may experience during our Centering Prayer period – including ideas, concerns, wandering imagination, distractions, noises, sensations of the body, perceptions, intuitions, and especially our thinking about our thinking, like when we say, "wow, I'm having a really great prayer time." Or, "this sucks, I can't believe all these thoughts I'm having. It's like a hail storm in my head."

To be "engaged" with our thoughts is an important distinction, in contrast to just "having thoughts." Or simply "being aware of thoughts." It's inevitable, normal, and even integral to have thoughts during the Centering Prayer period. It's inevitable because we are human and also conscious. Consciousness is that dynamic in us that gives us the capacity to know that we know, which is our normal way of being engaged with our thoughts.

And yet one of the things we can discover is that there is a difference between our consciousness seeing a thought so to speak in its mirror, reflecting it back to our awareness, and then reacting or interacting with that thought. In contrast, we can simply be with the thought in silence, or, be the still witness to the thought. Returning to the sacred word helps us develop the skill of simply being with whatever thoughts are observed without engaging with them.

In time, many will not need to return to their sacred word. We may discover, even if briefly, that we are simply present beyond the thoughts, even if there are thoughts. It's as if your awareness is underneath the thoughts, at a deeper level, which we call the spiritual level.

Thoughts are normal. Please don't think that because you are aware of your thoughts or engaged with your thoughts that you are a failure in this prayer method. Having thoughts and being engaged with your thoughts is normal. When you realize you are engaged with your thoughts, think nothing of it and simply return to your sacred word. Thoughts are also integral to the process of interior transformation and healing. This is because we usually aren't in control of what thoughts are coming up. Sometimes thoughts come up like old, buried shrapnel from a deep wound. Sometimes there will be tears and we will have no idea why. Sometimes there will be bodily pains or sensations or physical expressions such as coughs or muscle tightening. We call this experience "unloading."

All of this is the manifestation of thoughts in us, and this is integral to the interior healing process soaking in God's love. Our journey is going ever deeper into God's loving presence and grace and as we do so in the silence, the deep levels of unconscious and sub-conscious material, often stored in our body, start to loosen and come up.

The journey is up and out. As things come up, they are enabled to come out, and in some cases, just doing Centering Prayer twice a day for several months can be more therapeutic than years of therapy.

We may not understand what the thoughts are doing or saying to us in the Centering Prayer period. That is OK. Don't think about the thoughts. Be gentle with yourself. Just gently return to your sacred word and trust God knows what God is doing in your deepest level of being – a level beyond your own consciousness. The level of your soul, which is truly your embodied essence so very loved by God. The gentle interior action of returning to your sacred word is similar to mindfulness techniques of noticing and letting go.

Yet in Centering Prayer, we don't need to even really give much attention to noticing, we just return to our sacred word reaffirming our intention to consent to the deeper Reality that is possible, that we call "the presence and action of Holy Spirit." Over a period of about 20 minutes very often our brain waves begin to shift from normal Beta to more present and intuitive Gamma and Delta brain wave patterns. Amazingly, this is now measurable by fMRI (functional magnetic resonance imaging). This shift in brain wave function is the reason why, from a scientific perspective, there are so many positive side effects to most meditative methods. But it's not the reason we do Centering Prayer.

The interior gesture of returning to the sacred word is like a subtle tilting of the head downward to the heart. We don't say the sacred word with our mouth. We don't jam the sacred word up into our head. We don't react or get frustrated that we have to return to our sacred word again.

We just ever so gently return to our sacred word as a gesture of our consenting to the presence and action of God within our awareness. In the midst of this surrendering and returning, perhaps the awareness of a widening space may open in our solar plexus region, creating a sensation of peace. Physical sensations and experiences are different for everyone, but there is a widely reported experience following both individual and group Centering Prayer periods of a deepening peace and calmness in people – emotionally and physically.

It's a joy for me to observe a group of people at the beginning of an extended Centering Prayer retreat. At first, including myself, we often appear constricted and not at ease, very much up in their heads. However, by the end of the retreat, especially during the group sharing time, it's amazing to literally see the difference in people's bodies – they are more light, more grounded, more peaceful, and often times in awe of the deep rest and healing they experienced. As Thomas Keating reminds, in the world of Centering Prayer, anything is possible. And that is because it brings us so up close and personal to the presence and action of God's grace.

Guideline four:

> *At the end of the prayer period, remain in silence*
> *with eyes closed for a couple of minutes.*

Lest the deep rest of the 20 minutes of silence be disrupted too quickly or jarringly, give yourself some time to transition back to the world of Beta brainwaves and to the chores, children and traffic awaiting.

It's useful to set a timer with a gentle bell sound or nature sound to gently alert you that the prayer period is over. Such bells are now widely available as phone apps. This will allow you to fully surrender to the experience of prayer and not need to keep checking the clock to see if you have gone over or worry about how much time is left, which is often a powerful temptation at first. It's also very customary to end the prayer period by saying the Lord's Prayer, or something similar. This is especially helpful in a group Centering Prayer period. Often just the leader will say the prayer, slowly, allowing the circle of participants to gently come back into the room together. It's a threshold – moving from the deep silence into the world of our normal interactions. Take your time and cherish the interior rest that occurred during the 20 minutes of Centering Prayer.

Even if you don't feel anything, or even feel agitated, declaring you'll never do this again, don't assume that just because you were *not* aware of it that the Holy Spirit wasn't present and at work in you responding to your sincere efforts to consent to God's presence. God loves our consent and responds to it, just not always in the way we think, know or understand. This is God's mysterious way of personalized, pin-point precision grace.

Misperception #1:

Centering Prayer is "not Christian"

Centering Prayer is Christian because it's a practice in service to our deepening abiding in Christ (John 15.4) and Christ in us.

As such, the practice of Center Prayer helps us realize and remember, experience and feel the state Jesus invited us into. A state which he described as being one with God (John 17.23), or what is customarily called in the Christian tradition, the Unitive state.

Theologically, the Unitive state is simply a deepening of our being "in Christ," a condition St. Paul relies so heavily upon in his own writings and understanding of an individual's spiritual journey (e.g. 2 Corinthians 5.17). Later in the book, I'll describe in detail what is meant by the Unitive state.

Centering Prayer is not only Christian, it's also Trinitarian. The practice of resting in the silence deepens our interior experience with God through Christ by the presence and action of the Holy Spirit.

The method of Centering Prayer is designed to lead us into deeper surrender to God transcendent through Christ imminent by the Spirit omnipresent. What could be more beautiful? And what could be more Christian?

Presenting the practice of Centering Prayer in such a Trinitarian context reveals a threefold pattern grounded in grace, that births the primary theological virtues of hope, faith and love. Please notice:

The source of the practice is grace.

The inspiration of the practice is hope.

The effort of the practice is faith.

The effect of the practice is love.

The source of faith is not in oneself, but in the love of God. It's the love of God that we experience as an energy transforming us "by the renewing of our minds" (Romans 12.1) further into the image of Christ, which is being formed in us through the space for grace we call silence (Galatians 4.19).

Perhaps take a pause and re-read that last sentence. It's key: *It's the love of God that we experience as an energy transforming us "by the renewing of our minds" (Romans 12.1) further into the image of Christ, which is being formed in us through the space for grace we call silence (Galatians 4.19; Matthew 6.6).* The inspiration of the practice is hope that attracts us toward a deepening experience of the living Word of God and the silence beneath that radiant reality. Hope permeates through the darkness, calling our soul to simply be still and experience God (Psalm 42.10). We wait. We surrender. We consent. All contemplative dispositions that require and cultivate our hope in God.

The effort of the practice isn't a striving for or a promethean rising up toward a better self, but rather the humble effort of our will consenting in faith. It requires faith because there is often little tangible to the experience of Centering Prayer other than resting in the silence. The effort is truly about the intention of the will to consent to who and what God is for us and our transformation, something we may not be able to see or understand.

It's the kind of faith that is nurtured by increasing experiences of and with Christ, in the silence and in the sacrament. It's the kind of faith demonstrated by Mary who said in response to the angel's invitation to bear Christ into the world: "let it be in me according to your Word" (Luke 1.38). Thus, the effort of faith is uniquely connected to trusting in our unique and living encounter and experience of Christ in us.

The effects of the practice are ultimately the slow unloading of our interior wounds and baggage, and the self's transformation, like water into wine, into love itself. In other words, the primary effect is that we simply become love. Where there once might have been judgment, fear or anger, now there is love.

The Spirit in the silence is like a sponge, soaking up much in us that is un-loving and squeezing it out ever so gently, replacing it with a new way of being that is both simply and profoundly, in a word, love. Over time, one discovers that the practice of Centering Prayer is a deeper encounter with a sanctification by means of grace that leads to increased wholeness and healing, often releasing in and through our lives, in seemingly miraculous ways, the fruit and gifts of the Holy Spirit (Galatians 5).

So, a big-picture summary of the theological foundations of the practice and method of Centering Prayer leads us to say that Centering Prayer is a deepening journey that is:

An abounding *grace* grounded in the Trinity.

An attracting *hope* grounded in the Word of God.

An enduring *faith* grounded in the experience of Christ.

A divine *love* grounded in the presence of the Spirit.

Historically, Centering Prayer falls well within the general Christian contemplative tradition. It's kissing cousins with the well respected and universally accepted Christian practice of *lectio divina* – the slow, attentive spiritual practice of reading and listening to the scriptures. And just who might be kissing us?

Well, of course, it's the Spirit of God, who woos us into the abundant life in Christ through both love and suffering, or as St. Paul simply puts it, the "all things" of life (Romans 8.28ff). Centering Prayer is also not a new branch on the great tree of contemplative Christian prayer. While it's not identical to the teaching of the 14th Century anonymous book *The Cloud of Unknowing,* their similarities are obvious to most. For example, using one word to "pierce through the darkness" of silence as a gesture both of our consent to God, and desire for God.

The family tree of Centering Prayer can also be traced to the teachings of Christian masters such as Meister Eckhart, Theresa of Avila, John of the Cross and Thomas Merton. While none of these contemplatives taught the specific method of Centering Prayer, they all articulated the presuppositions of Centering Prayer, such as consenting to God, the need for unknowing, the role of silence in our spiritual journey, and the grace inspired destination of ever deeper Union with God through Christ by the Spirit until Christ is "all in all" (Colossians 3.11).

One of the reasons a particular method of meditative prayer was not more widely known within western Christianity until relatively recently, is that the method of meditative prayer was usually not taught in books. The method was often taught by oral tradition, usually in monastic settings.

It's also true that after the Enlightenment and Reformation, much of western Christianity threw the baby out with the bathwater, avoiding anything "mystical" in favor of everything "rational." Much has previously been written on that historical episode and the sad consequences of such an exclusive focus on rational theology and active spiritual practices to the exclusion of the mystical and contemplative.

Thankfully, a balance is returning, in part, because the church and its people are starving for spiritual depth. In our era, at a time when humankind desperately needs practical methods to help us in our world of division, fear and crisis, the doors of the monasteries opened and a beautiful gift was released – a simple method of generous scope, available to all.

If you are interested in reading more about the founding and history of the development of Centering Prayer, it has been widely written about by Father Thomas Keating, William Meninger and Basil Pennington, all three of whom were integral in "creating," teaching, and popularizing the prayer. Centering Prayer is also distantly related to the Jesus Prayer, a prayer method widely practiced in the Eastern Orthodox and Russian Orthodox Christian communions, and increasingly among Roman Catholics and protestants. While Centering Prayer and the Jesus Prayer are different methods of meditative prayer, they share the similarity of resting with God and using a brief word/sentence to "guard" the heart from the provocations of thoughts, feelings and perceptions we are all so prone to. In all the wisdom teachings, both East and West, it's widely agreed that spiritual growth requires dealing with the ceaseless, self-reflective, mechanical thoughts and feelings that arise in our mind-awareness and body-experience. The Jesus Prayer addresses this with some form of the phrase, *"Lord Jesus Christ, Son of God, have mercy upon me a sinner."* Centering Prayer addresses this by the consent to God's presence and action using an individually chosen "sacred word."

Centering Prayer is Christian because it's practiced by Christians. Prayer, words or music are not intrinsically Christian. These words only "become" Christian when spoken or sung *by* Christians. In a sense, they are sanctified by those who in good faith and obedience to God use a human method to surrender more of their self to God so that they might decrease and that Christ might increase

(John 3.30). Centering Prayer is Christian because the living Christ uses it by the Spirit to bear the fruit of righteousness and peace, transformation and healing, hope and love in countless lives.

Finally, Jesus taught us not to judge our neighbor. But Jesus also taught that you will know a tree by its fruits (Matthew 7.20). The fruit of Centering Prayer are none other than the fruit of the Spirit – such as love, joy, peace, patience and kindness (Galatians 5.22ff).

If such are some of the fruit of this beautiful prayer method, it might also be wise to remember Jesus' openess and freedom toward other spiritual teachers or different spiritual practices when he put it this way: "unless they are against me, they are for me" (Matthew 12.20). Centering Prayer is certainly for Christ. Perhaps that is enough reason for us to be open to Centering Prayer in our lives, families and churches. Hopefully, this clarifies both that and how Centering Prayer is a solidly Christian spiritual practice.

Misperception #2:

Centering Prayer is "not biblical"

Centering Prayer is as biblical as you want it to be. While the exact words "Centering Prayer" do not appear anywhere in the Hebrew or Christian Scriptures, the motivation toward, and purpose of Centering Prayer, do. For example, consider the possibilities of the following two passages: "be still and know that I am God" (Psalm 46.10) and "abide in me as I abide in you" (John 15.4).

Just because the method of Centering Prayer is neither explicitly outlined in the Bible nor taught by Jesus does *not* automatically disqualify it as a legitimate spiritual practice for Christian formation. If a step by step biblical description is needed to legitimate everything Christians do or believe, we would need to cease using the word Trinity, a word not explicitly found in the Bible.

Just because the Bible does not speak of a particular word or spiritual practice, does not make it inappropriate. If that were the case, the doctrines of the Trinity and Eucharist would both be far less clear than they are today due to the method of theological correlation and analogy developed over time through spiritual conversation and ecumenical councils.

Furthermore, the Bible does not speak of a great many important things which we now take for granted and value very highly, such as DNA, the expanding universe, treatments for cancer, the Internet, and most importantly as it relates to Centering Prayer, the existence of the unconscious and measurable different brain wave functions. Remember, Jesus said that his disciples could not "bear all that he had to teach" them (John 16.12), but that the Holy Spirit would come after his ascension and continue the teaching Jesus began by leading us "into all truth" (John 16.13). This means that there is a spiritual dynamic in place that allows for the developmental unfolding of knowledge and practice.

Remember, it took nearly four hundred years *after* Jesus' ascension for the church to generally agree upon the nature of Jesus' relationship to "God the Father" (at both the Council of Nicaea 325 C.E. and Chalcedon 451 C.E.). They called their resolution to the question the "hypostatic union;" a key element to the doctrine of the Trinity. But did Jesus ever speak of himself using this word? Absolutely not. He hinted at it in other ways (i.e. John 10.30).

Christian knowledge and practice is developmental. Grounded in the historical events of the Incarnation and the earliest Christian experiences with, and reflections about Jesus, Christian theologians and teachers have tirelessly sought to integrate faith and practice so to verify experience with Scripture.

There is not a universally accepted formula to do this. It requires listening. Discernment. Intuition. Wisdom. It's a developmental and relational process – which means that understanding emerges from the unknown into the known as led by the Spirit. We don't have a dead faith. It's living and active in and through us right now.

The Scriptures tell and the tradition teaches us what has been revealed and received. Yet, we do not know what will be. It's the Spirit of truth who leads us forward bringing about God's intended destiny for us and the cosmos. This requires trust and faith. For some, the lack of control over the process prompts fear – which will only hinder one's present and future flourishing in Christ, because fear is the opposite of love (1 John 4.18).

While fear is not an appropriate method for theological reflection, we are instructed to "test the spirits" (1 John 4.1). So, let us proceed to test the spirit of Centering Prayer. We'll do so by using the method of theological analogy to reveal the endless connections between the Scriptures, human motivation, and the general purpose of Centering Prayer, and in so doing, reveal the thoroughly biblical foundation for this good, true and beautiful gift of the Spirit for a spiritual age in transition, moving beyond old, unworkable, fear and control based doctrines into the life giving presence of love. We'll do this following three paths: Motivation, Purpose and Method.

Motivation: The Why – *Answering the question, "for what reason?"*

The motivation to practice Centering Prayer is grounded in the reality that human beings are created in the image of God (Genesis 1.26). The breath of God brought us into being (Genesis 2.7). We are ontologically connected with God and long for a fullness of awakening reunion. Thus, the Spirit bears witness to our spirit, as like calls to like. (Romans 8.5-16).

The longing for the fullness of reunion becomes all the more acute when we experience suffering, or discover, as Thomas Keating likes to say, that the way we have been looking for happiness in life is often in the wrong direction. Realizing this, we are given the opportunity to change our direction (literally, *metanoia*, meaning repent).

This shift in direction tends to lead us to seek for something deeper. Indeed, for the awareness and experience of Union so beautifully described by St. Paul as the promise that in Christ, "nothing can separate us from the love of God" (Romans 8.39). In Centering Prayer we remember and experience this truth again and again. This is not only our true happiness, it's also our enduring bliss.

In simple terms, Centering Prayer is motivated by the longing in the human soul for God (Psalm 42.1-3). The longing is a response to God's call. It's as if we are hearing beautiful and mysterious music from a distant room. We know it's calling to us. We feel it in every cell. Sometimes we are distracted by a conversation nearby. Sometimes we ignore the music. But it's profoundly present, singing its octave of adoration, shouting its hymns of glory, booming its timpani's of silent thunder. The music is sheer grace, drawing us to the reality of the truth which *is* love experienced through silent prayer. The experience of Centering Prayer is possible because of the grace of God flowing forth from the Center of the Trinity, one for another, and all for us – including the creation, earth, sea, sky and cosmos.

Such grace is true for all prayer practices. It's true for Centering Prayer *all the more* because the essence of our response to the call is total surrender. We surrender. We consent in silence to the presence and action of God. We cease trying to get to God, or from God something with our intercessions and complaints. We simply say "Yes" to God's "Yes" through the veil of silence.

We are motivated not to find God in the center of our being, but to find our center in the depth of God's love through Christ by the Spirit. Could there be anything more beautifully biblical than that?

Purpose: The Where – *Answering the question, "to what end?"*

The purpose of Centering Prayer is grounded in the reality that while we are created in the image of God, we are also "fallen." To be fallen suggests we were actually created to live at a higher level. Thus, we are in need of restoration, of transformation, understood as the therapeutic healing of our human nature in Christ. We recognize that to be in Christ is to be a "new creation" (2 Corinthians 5.17), reconciled to God with whom we are now at peace (Romans 5.1).

In addition to this new state of being with God through Christ, we are also invited into a deeper participation with Christ, indeed to participate in the "divine nature" (2 Peter 1.4). Traditionally, this is called the process of sanctification, and the goal of this journey of sanctification (purgation/illumination) is what the Western church calls "Union," and the Eastern church calls "Theosis," and what I simply call "becoming love."

Thus, it's fair to say that the purpose and end of Centering Prayer is love. Not the love of our Self, not even the love of God or neighbor, but the transformation into love. Remember, God is love (1 John 4.7-8), and we are children of God and heirs with Christ (Romans 8.12-17). Love is the God-intended destiny of the creation and Centering Prayer is simple, peasant-bread for our nourishment on this most holy and mysterious journey home into Christ. In the silence and in the surrender, we receive what we are to become: Love. Christ. God.

Method: The How – *Answering the question "what is the means to get there?"*

The method of Centering Prayer is grounded in the reality that the disciples of Jesus asked him how to pray (Luke 11.1-2). Their question gives us permission to continue to ask, seek and knock for the fullness of an answer. People have been doing so ever since the disciples first asked. In this most confusing era of human history, thanks to the tireless ministries of Father Thomas Keating, Father William Meninger, Father Basil Pennington, Father Carl Arico, Gail Fitzpatrick, Tim and Barbara Cook, the Contemplative Outreach organization, the Church of Conscious Harmony and many others, the method of Centering Prayer is widely known. These spiritual elders and beautiful communities have released from the heart of their contemplative dispositions, a simple tool for the blessing of all.

The method of Centering Prayer is grounded upon our intention. We express our intention to love, surrender, consent, follow, trust, believe, hear, listen, taste, see and know by simply sitting in silence and using a humble word to guard our heart and mind from its chatter and wandering. Intention. It's everything in the Christian journey. Intentional moments of surrender are modeled after the template of the Prodigal Son, who in a moment of intention "came to his senses" and returned home to the father (Luke 15.11-32), his temporal source of life and love.

It was a difficult journey home, and when he returned he discovered that his father had been waiting all along, probably sending out his own intention for the son's safe return. Somehow, the intentions met like magnets and the miracle of return occurred. Intention is completely different than attention, and this distinction makes all the difference in the fruits of the prayer. This template is all the more true for us, and our relationship with God, who is our Eternal Source. So, intention is the foundation of the method of Centering Prayer.

A common misconception about the method of Centering Prayer is that Jesus gave us the only method of prayer we need in the Lord's Prayer. While the Lord's Prayer provides a three-fold model for prayer (adoration, petition, contrition), it's not the sole end or method of all prayer. Word-based, discursive prayer, like the Lord's Prayer, over time often leads one to a deeper awareness of prayer beyond words to simply being with God (Psalm 46.10). John of the Cross, a 16th century contemplative and Christian mystic, summarized all the different kinds of prayer into two categories: discursive (with words) and contemplative (with an inner "seeing," beyond words).

Development or progress in prayer is often characterized by the slow transformation of our "wordy" prayers *into* silence. We simply rest before God's "I Am-ness," consenting with the wordless intention, Abba, "here I am" (Exodus 3.4; Isaiah 6.9), or with Mary's simple surrender, "let it be in me according to your word" (Luke 1.38).

The Word of God is the living presence of Christ conveyed by the Spirit through scripture, sacrament, nature and silence. The word "Word," from the Greek *Logos,* conveys the principle of intelligence: the form and function of Divine Mind imprinting and holding all of matter together by an energetic impulse of creative, erotic love, literally the wish for and manifestation of all things to be and become.

What was the Word of God who became flesh doing alone at night in prayer? Was the Word of God as the Eternal Word of God using words? What word would need to be spoken by the One Eternal Word that is all words? Ignatius, 2nd Century church father, said it best: silence was God's first word.

The method of Centering Prayer rests upon such ancient wisdom and as such also illuminates our own reading and understanding of the scriptures. So, in the end, not only is Centering Prayer biblical, it's also the very means to read the bible more deeply. But, not only that, it turns out beyond our reading of the bible, even more importantly, Centering Prayer facilitates the bible reading us. Through a daily Centering Prayer practice, we become more permeable to the Word of God, and we discover that the light shines in our own interior darkness, not to shame or frighten us, but to wake us up further and lead us deeper into the promise land of the life and love of God.

Misperception #3:

Centering Prayer is "dangerous"

Centering Prayer is not dangerous, but it can be disruptive. Centering Prayer is disruptive to the parts of us that wish to resist God's love and grace. These parts, psychologically speaking, might be called the unconscious programs for happiness that co-opt us for their own purposes. God's love wishes to heal and transform us and this often requires, what author Dallas Willard calls, a "renovation of the heart."

In the language of St. Paul, Centering Prayer is a practice that helps us to daily "die to self" (Romans 6.6-8) and to "put on the mind of Christ" (Philippians 2.5)." Such intentions will ultimately be disruptive to the hidden and subtle dimensions of our self that do not acknowledge God's utterly liberating and light-filled love. Such dimensions are often not detected in the normal dimness of our day-to-day activity because they remain embedded in the unconscious, or sub-conscious.

As St. John says, "the light shines in the darkness, but the darkness resists it" (John 1.5). One of the side effects of the practice of Centering Prayer is that such dimensions are revealed in the healing light of God's love. These dynamics are often purged, unloaded and reintegrated into our being by the presence and action of the Holy Spirit in the silence. Can God do this without Centering Prayer? Of course, but in our era of psychological awareness and intensified, stress filled lifestyles, God has blessed us with a renewal of contemplative prayer practices that have been a part of the Christian tradition from its earliest beginnings.

For example, Basil of Caesarea (330 – 379 C.E.) taught of the need for a continual mindfulness of God, remembering God in the silence of the heart. Basil represents just one point of light from an expansive and diverse tradition burning bright. The Tradition is trying to help us, not hurt us. In the deep rest and stillness of silence, we are freed to flourish into the fullness of our God intended destiny as "co-heirs with Christ" (Romans 8.17) and "participants of the divine nature" (2 Peter 1.4).

In Centering Prayer God continues the process. Centering Prayer is one way for us to experience all the riches of Christ so "to be renewed in the spirit of our minds, and to clothe ourselves with the new self, created according to the likeness of God in true righteousness and holiness" (Ephesians 4.23-24). If scripture and sacrament are the hands of sanctification, then silent prayer practices (such as Centering Prayer) are at least its servant feet, bearing us along step by step on our spiritual journey deeper into Christ. When considering the misperception that Centering Prayer is dangerous, it's also important to remember that Christianity is dangerous.

Recall what happened to Jesus. Or Stephen. Or countless ancient and current saints in the communion of faith. So, why might some think that Centering Prayer is dangerous? Why would some be fearful of this beautiful and harmless spiritual practice?

First, there is a fear that in the process of Centering Prayer we might "open our minds up" to harmful spiritual entities/energies.

In my experience, I don't need any help with this. There are already enough harmful, unloving, critical, judgmental, depressive thoughts *already in me*. The problem is that these thoughts are stuck in there. We need just such a practice as Centering Prayer to help us access the interior grace of surrender to the Spirit of God, who can and will release and heal us of our known and unknown negative thoughts and energies. Some form of meditative prayer is therefore part of the solution. I begin to increasingly recognize this during the silence of Centering Prayer. Thus, it's perfectly normal to begin to be uncomfortable with the random and sometimes *un-believable* thoughts that rise up in the mind and body in the silence. Most likely, these are not coming from an harmful "spirit" or entity outside of you, but from the unconscious, or what St. Paul called "the flesh."

That the thoughts are occurring does not make you bad. It makes you human. Thoughts are an invitation to rest with God and recognize that you don't know yourself as thoroughly as you thought, and that you are not in control either!   Sometimes the body has retained emotions from painful past experiences and the silence and deep rest of stillness allows the body to release that pain and stored tension. As contemplative teacher Father Carl Arico memorably puts it, the issues are in our tissues. As a result, sometimes it does feel like we are getting worse before we get better. This experience is what is referred to as the Divine Therapy.

Second, when we begin to observe the chatter of thoughts occurring in us, from time to time, we might think we are hearing voices, suggestions, and inner promptings. The best thing to do is to ignore them and gently return to the sacred word. Even if the thoughts are of a beautiful spiritual quality, the purpose of Centering Prayer is not to think about them; you can do that another time. If they are important God will remind you of them when you are finished praying. In my experience, most of the time, I end up forgetting about them; especially the thoughts that, at the time, seemed to be of great importance. On other occasions, the impressions or insights remained long after the prayer time ended and inevitably bore spiritual fruit in my life.

Centering Prayer is not dangerous, but it's disruptive. So, generally speaking, hearing voices or seeing images on the "screen" of the mind's imagination is of no concern. I say "generally" because, in the soul/psyche realm, there are always exceptions to the rule, such as in the case of a diagnosable mental illness or a chemically induced altered state of reality. In my experience, should one have a disturbing spiritual encounter at any point in life, whether in prayer or at work, in the firm witness of two centuries of Christian contemplative practice, Centering Prayer would be one of the safest places to be.

Should you experience disturbing or provocative thoughts in your meditative prayer, simply return to the sacred word and to your intention to consent to God, and love for God. During such difficulties with our thoughts, there may also be various physical or emotional feelings and manifestations, such as tears, tensions, arousals, or general uneasiness. In these moments, please know that there is nowhere safer than returning to your sacred word in the stillness and silence. The invitation to be still and receive God's grace is an invitation to sheer sanctuary, even amidst any agony. Take God up on the offer. You will never be the same, and perhaps you will love it.

Also, the name of Jesus Christ is always your shield in the silence. Remember, you are guarded by the power of grace through baptism, sacrament and, most of all, in your union with Christ by the Spirit through faith. Do not fear the silence. In Christ, nothing can separate you from the love of God – including the silence or any experiences in that silence, even if they are of a spiritual, emotional or disturbing nature.

If something is disturbing you, it's probably rising up from your unconscious because you need to be freed from it. In that case, simply know that the light of Christ shines in the darkness and brings freedom. As you observe that which disturbs, give it to God by simply returning in faith to the sacred word, letting God take care of the rest. Cry if you need to. Feel if you need to. Be with it. Be still and know that God is the God who is here with you. It's also ideal if you can share your journey with a wise and trusted spiritual companion.

Increasingly, pastors are discovering the gifts of Centering Prayer for themselves and the more this occurs, the more helpful they will be to others who may need spiritual counsel or guidance in dealing with something that has come up through the Centering Prayer process. If there is no one in your life who you trust enough to share, try visiting a Cistercian, Trappist or Camaldolese monastery, or writing to their Abbot for advice. Also, Contemplative Outreach offers many helpful resources and retreats and is an ideal way of meeting fellow spiritual pilgrims on the journey deeper into God's love through the silence. If you are in Austin, Texas, I highly recommend visiting the one contemplative church in the world I am aware of called The Church of Conscious Harmony.

Third, Centering Prayer can lead us to encounter difficult periods on the spiritual journey. Historically, these periods are called Dark Nights or times of "purgation," or simply being on "the cross." These have been classically described in the writings of John of the Cross, and do not need to be repeated here (I will explore them in a later chapter). The point of reminding us of this fact is that one should not interpret the process of interior purgation, transformation, sanctification or healing as *dangerous*, despite their difficulties. They are disruptive, yet integral to our spiritual growth and meant to further raise us up into the life of Christ (Romans 6.6-14).

Fourth, we do live in a spiritual world and prayer is the language of that world. Centering Prayer is a practice that speaks the language of silence. Remember, silence is only one form of prayer on the spectrum of prayer. It's no more dangerous than any other kind of prayer. Keep in mind, prayer is not limited to Christians. Most of the world's religions have some sort of prayer modality, including a meditative, silent expression. Prayer is one of the most universal and common manifestations of our humanity.

It's not the modality of prayer that is of concern, but rather the *intention* and *attention* of that prayer. *Why* we are praying and *to whom* we are praying are key questions to address in any discussion on prayer. In the case of Centering Prayer, we pray to and within the love of the Triune, Creator God and Abba of our Lord and Savior Jesus Christ because we wish to consent further to God's loving presence and action in our lives by the Holy Spirit to the praise of God's holy name.

In summary, children, youth and adults who are taught the practice of Centering Prayer should be assured that they are most safe in the silence with God. One reason this is so is because only God's Spirit searches the depths of our being and knows us beyond our own knowing when we are not thinking. The "demons," or provocations can only know what we *are* thinking. They cannot know what we are *not* thinking in the silence.

Anyway, under the shield of the name of Jesus Christ, rest in the deep silence with God, with the certainty that all things work together to the good for those who love Christ, our good shepherd who calls us by name, both in spoken word and in the silence.

Misperception #4:

Centering Prayer is about "finding the Divine inside you"

I understand why some might think that Centering Prayer is about finding the Divine "inside." Sometimes even the best intentions generate more confusion than clarity on this subject. Given the immensity and profundity of the subject matter, grace is required for all. We're all on such unique and personal journeys.

One way to begin to address the confusion surrounding this misperception, is to clarify our terms. The writings of the New Testament make it abundantly clear that the goal of the Christian life is union with God through Christ by the Spirit. Consider the following major passages on the subject:

"*I am the vine, you are the branches. Those who abide in me <u>and I in them</u> bear much fruit, because apart from me you can do nothing.*" (John 15.5)

"*Set your minds on things that are above, not on things that are on earth, for you have died, and <u>your life is hidden with Christ in God</u>.*" (Colossians 3.3)

"*It is no longer I who live, but it is <u>Christ who lives in</u>*

me." (Galatians 2.20)

"*My little children, for whom I am again in the pain of childbirth until Christ is formed in you.*" (Galatians 4.19)

"*I pray that, according to the riches of his glory, he may grant that you may be strengthened in your inner being with power through his Spirit, and that Christ may dwell in your hearts through faith, as you are being rooted and grounded in love. I pray that you may have the power to comprehend, with all the saints, what is the breadth and length and height and depth, and to know the love of Christ that surpasses knowledge, so that you may be filled with all the fullness of God.*" (Ephesians 3.16-19)

"*Thus he has given us, through these things, his precious and very great promises, so that through them you may escape from the corruption that is in the world because of lust, and may become participants of the divine nature.*" (2 Peter 1.4)

"*So we have known and believe the love that God has for us. God is love, and those who abide in love abide in God, and God abides in them.*" (1 John 4.16)

In addition to the Bible, the Church fathers – ancient and modern – also bear witness to the truth of God's inward presence and our experience of union with God. Let's begin with the writings of John of the Cross.

In his seminal book *The Ascent of Mount Carmel*, John of the Cross explains the nature of this union with God. He writes:

"To understand the nature of this union, one should first know that God sustains every soul and dwells in it substantially, even though it may be the greatest sinner in the world. This union between God and creatures always exists. By it God conserves their being so that if the union would end they would immediately be annihilated and cease to exist. Consequently, in discussing union with God, we are not discussing the substantial union which always exists, but the union and transformation of the soul in God. This union does not always exist, but we find it only where there is likeness of love. We will call it "the union of likeness," and the former "the essential or substantial union." The union of likeness is supernatural, the other natural. The supernatural union exists when God's will and the soul are in conformity, so that nothing in the one is repugnant to the other. When the soul completely

rids itself of what is repugnant and un-conformed to the divine will, it rests transformed in God through love."[1] In other words, John of the Cross is speaking here of the path of sanctification through the practice of contemplation and love.

While all human beings share in a certain union with God as created in God's image (i.e., the substantial union), not all human beings share in the transformational union, which is rooted in our union with God through Christ by the Spirit, activated by faith, baptism, sacraments and the means of grace, such as prayer.

In Christ, we are invited to follow the narrow path of surrender of self so to be full of God, or as John the Baptist put it, that Christ might increase and I might decrease (John 3.30). One way in which we follow Christ deeper into this transforming union is through the practice of meditative prayer. John of the Cross goes on to use a helpful common analogy about the process of sanctification, or what he terms our "transformative union:"

"Here is an example that will provide a better understanding of this explanation. A ray of sunlight shining

upon a smudgy window is unable to illumine that window completely and transform it into its own light. It could do this if the window were cleaned and polished. The less the film and stain are wiped away, the less the window will be illumined; and the cleaner the window is, the brighter will be its illumination. The extent of illumination is not dependent upon the ray of sunlight, but upon the window. If the window is totally clean and pure, the sunlight will so transform and illumine it that to all appearances the window will be identical with the ray of sunlight and shine just as the sun's ray. Although obviously the nature of the window is distinct from that of the sun's ray (even if the two seem identical), we can assert that the window is the ray or light of the sun by participation."[2]

The key point here is that our union with God through Christ by the Spirit occurs through participation and can range in intensity and comprehensiveness dependent upon our willingness to be transformed through our surrender to God's presence and action in us. Centering Prayer is one means of grace we have of consenting to God's cleansing and healing process.

In John's analogy, please note that we do not become the

holy, Triune, creator God of heaven and earth (i.e., the light). We simply become heirs with Christ (Romans 8.17) and participants of the divine nature of Christ through faith (2 Peter 1.4). Our consent in faith enables us also to become continuing witnesses to Christ as lights in the world, bearing the love of God in word, deed and silence as the ongoing mission to the ends of the earth (Acts 1.9).

Renowned Roman Catholic monk and popular spiritual writer of the 20th Century, Thomas Merton, further conveys the tradition of participation like this:

"In order to know and love God as He is, we must have God dwelling in us in a new way, not only in His creative power but in His mercy, not only in His greatness but in His littleness, by which He empties Himself and comes down to us to be empty in our emptiness, and so fill us in His fullness...by supernatural missions of His own life. The Father, dwelling in the depths of all things and in my own depths, communicates to me His Word and His Spirit. Receiving them I am drawn into His own life and know God in His own Love, being one with Him in His own Son. Discovery of my identity begins and is perfected in these

missions, because it is in them that God Himself, bearing in Himself the secret of who I am, begins to live in me not only as my Creator but as my other and true self ("I live, now not I, but Christ lives in me").[3]

Notice the clear distinction in Merton: the oneness with God is through the "Son;" this makes all the difference! There is an eternal distinction between the upward path of self-realization through evolutionary ascent through levels of consciousness, and the path of grace inviting us into divinization and self-surrender in Christ, becoming a participant in the Divine nature.

Furthermore, any "true self" is not my own, but is a gift from God through Christ, which is my life, "in whom I live and move and have my being" (Acts 17.28).

It's not just Roman Catholic theologians who share this perspective of our interior experiences of union with God through Christ.[4] For example, here is the "mystical union" perspective of Protestant reformer John Calvin:

"Therefore . . . that indwelling of Christ in our hearts – in short, that mystical union — accorded by us the highest

degree of importance, so that Christ, having been made ours, makes us sharers with him in the gifts with which he has been endowed. We do not, therefore, contemplate him outside ourselves from afar . . . but because we put on Christ and are engrafted into his body – in short, because he deigns to make us one with him. For this reason, we glory that we have fellowship of righteousness with him."[5]

The tradition of participation and interior union with God through contemplative silence is even present in such Protestant stalwarts as Karl Barth, who once wrote:

"Confronted with the mystery of God, the creature must be silent; not merely for the sake of being silent, but for the sake of hearing. Only to the extent that it attains to silence, can it attain to hearing. But, again, it must be silent not merely for the sake of hearing, but for that of obeying. For obedience is the purpose and goal of hearing. Our return to obedience is indeed the aim of free grace. It is for this that it makes us free. It is for this that it confronts us as mystery."[6]

By "hearing" I take Barth to be speaking of what Thomas Keating calls our "consent" to God's presence and action in the simple act of faith and relationship that is Centering Prayer.[7] Adam Neder, a Barthian scholar, suggests in his recent book *Participation in Christ,* that there are certain and clear distinctions between the Barthian view of participation and those of Eastern Orthodoxy and St. John of the Cross. Nonetheless, Neder convincingly shows how participation is still an important and consistent theological theme in Barth's writings. Neder summarizes:

"God shares God's life with human beings in a way that is appropriate for them as creatures who are not, and never will become, the Lord of the covenant. Since Jesus Christ has secured this fellowship by fulfilling the covenant of grace, fellowship with God can never be abstracted or disconnected from him. He can never be left behind. [The creature] is neither the starting point for, nor the entrance into some supposedly higher or deeper form of union with God. Nor does the character of this fellowship evolve into some other form of relationship than that between Lord and servants. For Barth, union with God means union with Christ."[8]

Note that this Protestant perspective squares with the first principle that we are *not* the source of our union with God.

We consent to God's presence and action in us through our union with Christ by the Spirit.

Having surveyed a few important theological voices on the subject of our "interior" experience of God or "participation" with God through Christ, and having learned of its important place within the Christian tradition, let's now turn to the effect of contemplative prayer and how this practice helps one discover and fully participate in the truth of, and invitation to God's interior presence. In their helpful book on contemplative prayer, modern contemplatives Francis Kelly Nemeck and Marie Theresa Coombs, outline the effect of sustained contemplative prayer practices:

"The first and principal effect of contemplation is the experience of God within oneself. This is the very core of contemplation: the fact that God himself from within the soul directly and immediately communicates himself to it in love. And the second principal effect is like the first: namely, God communing with the soul in love elicits the soul's loving response causing it to commune with him. These are the first effects of contemplation in the ontological order (the order of being), but not necessarily in the

psychological order (the order of awareness of the soul)."[9]

Read in light of the Gospel passage "abide in me and I abide in you" (John 15.5), "finding God within" through contemplative prayer is the essence of the Christian revelation of the Trinity in the gospel of Jesus Christ. The good news is that in Christ by the Spirit, we can participate more fully in the presence and action of God leading us deeper into love and union, or in Jesus' terminology, into the kingdom of God.

To sum up: yes, Centering Prayer teaches that human beings can experience an interior deepening of relationship with God through the consistent practice of contemplative prayer. However, Centering Prayer does not teach that you or your "true self" is God. The creature cannot be God just as much as the window cannot be the light. However, there is a profound participation and oneness that can occur through our union with Christ by the Spirit in the silence.

This union begins as a simple relationship through faith and continues to realms that are beyond description. In the process, our "false self" (i.e. the old human nature of Romans 5-6) is revealed and healed in union with Christ (Colossians 3.9), and we are raised further into our "true life" in Christ (Romans 6.1-11), who, in the silence, transforms us "from one degree of glory to the next" (2 Corinthians 3.18).

All forms of prayer presuppose that the one praying is not God. If you were God why in the world would you need to pray? God praying to God? That's nonsense. Why would you need any spiritual practice at all? No amount of praying, whether discursive or meditative, will turn you into God or create the Divine within you. Centering Prayer will facilitate the union of the divine nature with your human nature, which we call Christ.

However, one of the gifts of Centering Prayer is that it can prepare you for a deeper participation with God so that you might discover, with the Apostle and many others, that more of your life is hidden with God in Christ (Colossians 3.1-4) until all there is – is Christ, your "all in all" (Colossians 3.11). When this occurs, it's normal to discover such well-known statements as personally true: *God is as close as my jugular vein.* Or, *I don't know where*

I end and God begins. These are ways of speaking, from the human perspective, that attempt to capture the experience of union in and with God. Until the Holy Spirit begins to spontaneously heal us of our deep, unconscious, repressed motivations driving our unloving behavior, moods, thoughts, words and deeds we will most likely need spiritual practices, or means of grace, to help us receive and consent to God's healing presence and action within. If we did not have such a difficulty with the "old nature" or "false self," and if we were not so wounded by the experience of living in this world, our transformation might occur simply by "believing" that Jesus died for our sins. I have not found it to be so easy.

But the way is simple. As simple as saying Yes to the silence, and from there the silence will do it's mysterious and lovely thing. The church and planet earth would be served by each Christian increasing their daily prayer practice and beginning a meditative prayer practice. Prayer is one of the greatest gifts we have been given to receive more of Christ's benefits. At just the right time in human history, the practice of Centering Prayer emerged as a simple method for the masses to help us cope with the stressors of life and move humankind further toward the fullness of the kingdom of God.

On a personal note, in the common language of my Protestant tradition, my "conversion" experience united me with God through Christ. However, it did not stop me from acting out my unconscious programs for happiness, such as fear, control, demand for beauty, greed, or lust, resulting in much pain for myself and others.

For years, even as a Christian and as a pastor, I consistently made a mess of my life by not seeking the kingdom of God first, nor loving God with all of my heart and strength. Difficulties emerged, sometimes as a result of living in disobedience to God's Word and Wisdom, and other times, as a result of simply being spiritually lazy – much of the time quite unconscious of the fact or even aware of my hidden, self-bound motivations.

My Protestant "justified by faith alone" attitude gave me every excuse to rest in my "blessed assurance" of salvation while blissfully ignoring my unconscious, harmful, unloving ways of thinking, feeling, speaking, acting and living. I can't be the only one. Slowly, over several years, my discursive prayer life led me quite unexpectedly and naturally to silent contemplation, and then to the formal method of Centering Prayer, and open to the gift of contemplation itself. I give thanks to God for the way in which this simple daily practice of consenting to God in the silence is a means of grace to me and many others, conveying more of the healing and transformation I have longed for my whole Christian life.

Misperception #5:

Centering Prayer is "Eastern Meditation"

Centering Prayer is not Eastern Meditation because it's a method of prayer formulated by several Roman Catholic Trappist Monks using principles drawn from the Christian monastic and historic contemplative prayer tradition.

Centering Prayer is also shaped by such primary Christian writers as John of the Cross, the unknown author of *The Cloud of Unknowing*, and other Christian teachers such as Theresa of Avila, Meister Eckhart, Thomas Merton, and such books as *The Philokalia*, and such spiritual practices as the Jesus Prayer, Hesychia, Watchfulness, *Lectio Divina*.

Just because a certain prayer practice also occurs in other religions or spiritual traditions does not make it an inappropriate practice. For example, prayer occurs in all or most of the world's major religions. So, in a sense, one could also say that intercessory prayer is just Hindu devotional prayer in the guise of Christian language. The argument dissipates in silliness.

Even if Centering Prayer *were* just Eastern Meditation re-clothed in Christian terminology what would be wrong with that? Where is there a scriptural prohibition against such meditative prayer? Drinking tea is an Eastern tradition but that did not stop the English from adopting it. Are all the Anglicans wrong to be drinking tea like the Buddhists and Hindus? Or, is the Queen now a Buddhist? Of course not. And you can see how silly this kind of guilty by association logic can get! In fact, how wonderful for Western Christianity, so stuck in the dogmatic, rationalistic head, to re-discover a vibrant spirituality below the neck. And thanks be to God for all the new inter-spiritual conversations now occurring as a result of many spiritual teachers courageous conversations and dialog.

The existence and practice of silent, meditative prayer occurs in all monotheistic, polytheistic and non-theistic, New Age and even secular spiritual traditions. No one tradition can claim meditation or contemplative prayer as their own. It belongs to the human family. Prayer and even meditative prayer is a birth-right expression of the human soul longing for God. Of course, each tradition teaches its perspective on the purpose, motivation and method of meditation.

Furthermore, no one has a problem with prayer in general

(i.e. intercessory, petitional, adorational, confessional, thanksgiving, etc.) Yet, there is significant reason to conclude that such prayer is essentially a particular *type* of meditation. Prayer is a practice of steadfast attention and devotion, which is at heart the definition of meditation. No doubt there are differences (e.g. addressed to a deity, reverent submission, etc.), but prayer in general is an aspect of meditation. Having begun with the universality of meditative prayer, let's move toward the specific. In what ways is Centering Prayer both unique and similar to Eastern meditation?

The uniqueness of Centering Prayer

The most important characteristic that differentiates Centering Prayer from other meditative prayer practices or mindfulness techniques is that its focus is primarily upon the intention to consent to God's presence and action.

Centering Prayer is a first step toward meditative prayer. Its fourfold method was designed especially for lay people to begin to explore the contemplative dimension of their Christian faith and experience, a gesture of total faith rooted in an intention to love and know the Triune God.

The second uniqueness of Centering Prayer is the emphasis that it's a relationship with God through Christ by the Spirit. Resting in God, listening to God, being silent to and with God is an invitation to a deeper intimacy with God. The intimacy occurs through our participation in the mystery of the Trinity – not just an energy field, or higher consciousness, or even not the universe itself, as wonderful as all three realties might be. They are all manifestations and "atmospheres" of God's energy, but they are not God. That is the fundamental Christian distinction in how we view ultimate reality. Reality is a manifestation of God's loving creativity, and participates in God's relationality – and yet that which is manifested is *not* the One which manifests.

The third uniqueness of Centering Prayer is that the effectiveness of the prayer is not dependent upon doing it "right." The effectiveness is rooted in total grace. God, by the Spirit, works through the silence to bring about healing and transformation in just the ways we need, even if we don't know what we need!

In fact, Centering Prayer is wedded to John of the Cross' understanding of the spiritual journey as a series of Dark

Nights. In this sense, Centering Prayer is a means of purgation on our way to illumination and union with God.

If you are interested in understanding the further uniqueness of Centering Prayer in contrast to other meditative prayer practices, please see such helpful books as:

Carl Arico's, *Taste of Silence: A Guide to the Fundamentals of Centering Prayer.*

Cynthia Bourgeault's, *Centering Prayer and Inner Awakening,*

David Frenette's, *The Path of Centering Prayer: Deepening Your Experience of God.*

Basil Pennington's, *Centered Living: The Way of Centering Prayer.*

The Similarity of Centering Prayer

Centering Prayer is similar to the other meditative prayer practices physiologically. Significant scientific research demonstrates the similarities of effect and function of meditation. Brain, mind and consciousness studies are con firming the important role meditative prayer can play in our general well-being and ongoing psychological development in life.

Centering Prayer is similar to other meditative prayer practices in that it helps people both enter into a more relaxed disposition through a basic focusing technique. In the case of Centering Prayer, the "sacred word." Methodologically, some have suggested that Centering Prayer is similar to Transcendental Meditation in that it shares the method of closing one's eyes and using a mantra for 20 – 30 minutes a day. While the two methods do share that in common, there are significant differences, chief of which is the role of the Trinity in Centering Prayer. Technically, the method of Centering Prayer also is a hybrid of the two traditional types of meditation: receptive meditation and concentrative meditation. Michael Washburn, in his book *The Ego and the Dynamic Ground* suggests that in receptive meditation the meditator,

"maintains the stance of an open and unmoving witness. Whatever emerges in or before the mind is observed crisply but not in any way acted upon or reacted to. The

images, feelings, and thoughts that present themselves to consciousness are witnessed uninterruptedly and with full consciousness but without in any way being engaged. In reflective meditation, the meditator emulates the character of a polished mirror, which reflects objects clearly, without becoming involved with them."[10]

Examples of this method are *satipatthana* (mindfulness) and *vipassana* (insight) meditations of Buddhism and *Zazen* of Zen.

In concentrative meditation, the meditator "selects a specific object, idea, or other reference datum and focuses undivided attention upon it. This focal datum can be either an external object or an internal content (e.g., a sensation, image, or idea)."[11] Examples of concentrative meditation are Pantanjali's *raja yoga*, the *jana* (absorption) of Buddhism and the *koan* exercises of Zen.

Popularly, Eckhart Tolle's *The Power of Now* also seems to use this moment as a focus point to help us get underneath our thoughts. The focusing method also has similarities to the meditative tradition of Jewish Hassidic scripture mantras or Sufi poetry.

Having said that, it's important to note the important role Centering Prayer has played in the development of inter-religious dialog and what is now called inter-spirituality post Vatican II. Prayer, especially silent prayer, is one place the currently conflicted major world religions can gather in unity and peace. Some may not think this necessary or good. Others do.

It seems to me that the transformation of our religious world views more toward unity and love is one key to the future flourishing of the human species and this extraordinary planet we call home. In summary, just because Centering Prayer falls within the technical similarities of these other well-known meditation methods does not make it non-Christian, wrong, dangerous or even "ungodly." That would be like saying modern evangelism is wrong because it seems to share some technical similarities to secular sales and marketing.

Centering Prayer is a totally appropriate and Christian prayer practice and is not guilty by association because it shares similarities of method or effect. Such similarities have more to do with human nature and being created in the image of God than any sinister plot to foil the Christian church or gospel in favor for some magical one world utopia of ohhmms. May it be agreed that Centering Prayer consents to the authority of the living Christ by the power of the Spirit, praying in silence and with the words, "thy kingdom come on earth as it is in heaven." What could be more beautiful, sacred and Christian than that! Enjoy!

Beyond Misperceptions:

Contemplative, Unitive and Centering Prayer

*H*aving clarified several misperceptions about Centering Prayer, let's go a little deeper by exploring the larger terrain that the daily practice of Centering Prayer may lead you into, namely contemplative experiences and the Unitive state.

While it's necessary and understandable to want to figure out the mystery of our spiritual experiences, or even to make "analytical" sense of the unfamiliar aspects of Centering Prayer, the essence of the prayer is ultimately to help us sink into the ultimately incomprehensible presence of love and life beyond the self-reflective and critical mind. So, let's start with the big picture of what we mean by the term "contemplative."

Contemplative

The word "contemplative" is frequently used as an umbrella term that summarizes the passive, receptive, and silent forms of spiritual life and prayer that are often associated with the monastic ethos, but certainly not limited to it. The contemplative experience is sometimes presented, unfairly so, in contrast or opposition to the active life. In such characterizations, the active life is exemplified by someone like Martin Luther King, Jr. who actively and publically worked for social justice. Whereas the contemplative life is often portrayed by Thomas Merton, an author and monk, who, while concerned for social justice spent much of his adult life writing in solitude, silence and prayer alone in a hermitage. In truth, both spiritual leaders drew upon the active and the contemplative dimension for their profound work and enduring impact. So, there is often more harmonization between the active way and the contemplative way than one might at first suspect.

Combined, the contemplative and active ways represent the full spiritual experience of Christian life that includes both the way of negation and the way of affirmation; the way of unknowing and the way of knowing; the way of silence and the way of words. Technically, these two ways are called the *apophatic*, representing the contemplative, and *kataphatic,* representing the active. We might say that these mutually wonderful and unique ways are the two beams of the one cross, or, to use a different analogy, two different sides of the one "widow's might" coin.

A famous biblical example of these polar, yet equally important sides of the Christian journey are the Mary (contemplative) and Martha (active) ways described by Jesus when he says to Martha, "you are worried and distracted by many things, but Mary has chosen the *better* part" (Luke 10.42). Perhaps a more helpful translation of the word "better," would be "appropriate." In other words, it's as if Jesus is saying to active Martha, "given the presence of Christ in your midst, at this moment, a more appropriate response for you is to be still; to be silent, and to know beyond knowing who I am, and discover who you are, and who you can become in my presence." It's not that Jesus is saying silence and stillness are the *only* ways or more "spiritual" ways. Rather, it's that Jesus is reminding us of the order of our spiritual fruitfulness.

First we plant the seed, then we fertilize the seed, and from there the seed grows into its full form of bearing good fruit. In other words, from that centered and renewed place of contemplative silence and stillness, knowing and being known, all sorts of ministry and active mission can and will flow, bearing beautiful and enduring spiritual fruit in appropriate ways, at appropriate times. However! First, let your Being come to completion for this moment in the presence of God. Like a seed in the soil, let stillness and silence be the atmosphere in which you recognize the appropriate way to be and then act. Recall how Jesus put it: "unless a grain of wheat falls into the earth and dies, it remains just a single grain; but if it dies, it bears much fruit" (John 12.24). Thus the contemplative way invites us to be *before* doing. And it's our being and dying to self in the silent love of God that is our deepest truth and safest refuge. Again, that's not to say that our doing can't shape and transform our being. It most certainly can and does. What we are drawing our attention to is that the invitation from Jesus is simply to recognize that there is an order to our inward journey: first being, then doing. From there, most certainly our doing will inform our being and our being will inform our doing, just as Frank Sinatra reminds us, singing "do-be-do-be-do."

Mary and Martha; the contemplative and active; being and doing. They are meant to go hand in hand, and are beautifully wed in the daily practices of the church throughout the world. And yet, far too many of us experience Christianity and our personal lives, as out of balance – perhaps too much active Martha without enough contemplative Mary! Too much busyness, yet too little stillness. So much stress, yet so little peace. Way too much doing without enough being.

Add to that our unconscious and repressed "False Self," or "Me Dynamic" and the situation often becomes a prescription for spiritual burn-out, inauthenticity, or reactive leadership. Notice that these dynamics in a spiritual community also foster the tendency to focus on religious or political controversies and doctrines rather than on the experience of being transformed into love together and as individuals. Perhaps you have also observed how Churches and individuals will do everything else *but* the one thing necessary Jesus speaks of, and as a result very little changes in our lives and communities.

For many of us, we discover that left unchecked, our "Self-Center" casts long shadows over our ordinary human condition and busyness. Unconsciously, this "falseness" within us resists the transforming light of God. We'll try everything else first before surrendering to God in the silence and stillness. No wonder people will pay thousands of dollars to take a vacation or go to the spa, just to experience a little peace and reprieve from the stresses of doing so much good! Alas, the goodness of the contemplative invitation! The long lost contemplative beam of our beloved cross of transformation can provide you all the rest and renewal you can imagine and need in very sustainable and gentle ways. Yet never forget it's a cross. And the contemplative cross will require and request of you your time and attention, and perhaps even your own Gethsemane tears of surrender. Please know this deeply: there is nothing wrong about being active or enjoying life, work and family in the world. Like Martha, it's completely normal and appropriate to be actively engaged in the world and concerned about others.

Yet, sometimes, this active energy and lifestyle is both the source of great fulfillment as well as the roadblock to continued spiritual growth. We may need to be in the world, but we may also need a little less of it in us. Like all good things, our active ministry and spiritual life can be subtly self-focused: one is getting something from it. If we are honest, sometimes it's more about us than it's about God.

So, in the mystery of God's grace, in order for us to grow deeper in the spiritual life, sometimes those perfectly appropriate active ways of being, and the personal pleasures and benefits one gets from that way of being, are unexpectedly taken away; perhaps just for a time, or sometimes more permanently. It's at these points of significant "spiritual pruning" in life, often connected with difficult major life events or unexpected transitions, that many people experience deep doubt about God; the waning of their initial spiritual zeal; the appearance of apathy, or even the diminishment of their care for God, themselves and others.

When we're not getting the normal "strokes" or personal "pleasure" from our "spiritual life" or service to others that we used to experience so effortlessly, we *then* get to see what our real motivation is on the spiritual journey. And this inner seeing and revelation of our motivation reveals who we are. And seeing this interior truth is a major part of the grace of any season of vulnerability, requiring great courage and trust in the God who is more interested in transforming you into Christ than about you feeling wonderful about being you.

At such times of potential inner growth, it's crucial for us to be able to see ourselves for who and what we are, and release it back to God in a joyful surrender, so that we can receive from God the ongoing "wound of love" that sometimes, in that moment or season of pruning, feels like the crushing agony of abandonment.

For this, we will need a sense of humor. We can't take ourselves too seriously, since, in the end, God's seems to be interested in loving our Self open, so that it's no longer just ours, but is also God's.

This phase of pruning and abandonment has traditionally been called purgation, and when it's more sustained, it's called a *Dark Night,* which may also be followed by other periods of deeper transformation (e.g. Active/Passive Nights of Senses and Active/Passive Nights of Spirit). The classic terminology about this process was popularized by St. John of the Cross, a 16th Century contemplative author, who wrote of his personal experiences on the spiritual journey in several of his books, the best known of which is *The Ascent of Mount Carmel.* The insights of St. John of the Cross continue to deeply resonate today, especially through the modern witness and writings of contemplative Bernadette Roberts.

In the midst of a Dark Night, it's as if God is asking unbearable questions of us, such as: *Will you love me now? Will you be spiritual now, when you seemingly get nothing out of it? Can you bear this cross? Can you trust me now even when you can't feel or know me like you used to?*

If one doesn't despair in the Dark Night and continues saying "Yes" to God's grace, and "Yes" to God helping you move through the darkness and difficulty despite even not knowing or feeling God's presence, even in the silence and stillness, a deeper dimension of strength and growth will be revealed in you through the suffering and darkness. In the light of this unseen strength you will be empowered to live more fully beyond that self-center, indeed beyond and in spite of your conscious and unconscious awareness of anything.

And, in place of your self-center that is grounded in consciousness, an enduring, unmovable center of love will emerge (as like the aperture of an eye widening) – a center of "nothingness" that is grounded in the Spirit of God. An empty center of sheer loving Presence around which will unwind and unfold all further growth. This undoing of the experiential self, layer by layer is actually the essence of the Christian journey of sanctification, moving through the external cross (i.e., events and seasons of suffering) to the internal transfiguration and resurrection (Romans 5 – 8), until one reaches the "full stature of Christ" (Ephesians 4.13), where perhaps even the ascension awaits us!

As we consider and seek to perceive these profound spiritual realities and processes in our lives, it may be helpful to remember that the English word "contemplative" is related to an expanded inward purity of perception for knowing, but not the kind of knowing we usually think of that is "intellectual" or "rational." The word "contemplative" comes from the Latin *Contemplatio,* which was often used to translate the Greek word *Theoria.* Contemplative scholar Andrew Louth describes the subject this way:

"The word *theoria* is derived from a verb meaning to look, or to see: for the Greeks, knowing was a kind of seeing, a sort of intellectual seeing. Contemplation is, then, knowledge, knowledge of reality itself, as opposed to knowing how: the kind of know-how involved in getting things done. To this contrast between the active life and contemplation there corresponds a distinction in our understanding of what it is to be human between reason conceived as puzzling things out, solving problems, calculating and making decisions, referred to by the Greek words *phronesis* and *dianoia,* or in Latin by *ratio* – and reason conceived as receptive of truth, beholding, looking, referred to by the Greek words *theoria* or *Sophia* or *nous* (intellect), or in Latin *intellectus.* Augustine expressed this distinction by using *scientia* for the kind of knowledge attained by ratio, and *sapientia*, wisdom, for the kind of knowledge received by *intellectus*. Human intelligence operates at two levels: a basic level concerned with doing things, and another level concerned with simply beholding, contemplating, knowing reality."[12] Dr. Louth's description cannot be improved upon, except to add that Jesus also famously invites us to a deeper way of seeing, though doing so using a different word than *theoria*. Jesus put it this way: "blessed are those who are pure in heart, for they shall *see* God" (Matthew 5.8).

So it seems, broadly speaking, that the contemplative practices of silence and some form of meditative resting prayer is the primary disposition and means by which people begin to deepen their spiritual life and move from just thinking or knowing about God rationally, to experiencing God, and beyond experience, to simply being with God so to see God – in all things, in all people and even in our own being.

It turns out silence is the universal language that facilitates such an interior and communal experience of perception (i.e. contemplation), because it purifies our hearts with God's love. Through our journey into the stillness of silence, we discover experiences of seeing beyond knowing; of knowing beyond seeing; of simply being beyond doing into the mind of Christ. Historically, much of what we understand as "contemplative" comes to us through the witness and experiences of the monastic tradition. Particularly influential was the desert mothers and fathers in the 3rd and 4th centuries C.E., in Northern Egypt, led by St. Anthony the Great. Then, similarly, later in the 6th century C.E. with the monastic renewal movement at Monte Cassino in Southern Italy under the leadership of St. Benedict of Nursia.

A movement which would eventually deeply imprint other monastic communities such as the Cistercian and Trappist monastic orders. Perhaps one of the most important gifts the monastic tradition has given Christianity is their focused way of life within the monastic setting. Through this intentional spiritual life in community, the church was able to identify the "ordinary milestones" of a Christian's spiritual development. For example, it became very clear to many that the spiritual journey started with some sort of conversion, continued with a period of training and reformation of life, including practical and ascetic disciplines that helped purify one's heart, mind, and body.

After a time, this purification led one to a season of illumination and deepened understanding, where one often began to see visible spiritual fruits, such as increased love, joy or peace in one's life. This season of illumination could then culminate in the Unitive state, which is another way of saying the "contemplative state." The terms are essentially synonymous, however it's important to recognize that while one may have contemplative experiences, one may not yet be in the Unitive state. It's understood that while experiences are temporary, states are more permanent. It's also important to remember that on the spiritual journey we don't work for results. We simply say "Yes" to God, and let God carry us further along in the great River of Life to wherever our unique destiny is to lead us.

Unitive

Having said that, though, the Unitive state is customarily reached on the spiritual journey through some participation and embodiment of contemplative practices such as silence, stillness, or meditative prayer. Yet, to be clear, you can be a contemplative without being in the Unitive state. You can also be in the Unitive state without being a contemplative. There is nothing that says there is only one path to the Unitive state. God uses all ways of being and all personality dispositions to facilitate our ongoing spiritual growth. Nor is there anything that says you have to be a contemplative Christian or that you must enter the Unitive state.

What is clear from the living tradition, is that the contemplative tools of silence and stillness seem to be the primary "atmosphere" God uses for both our undoing and our healing; for our illumination and our transformation. And who would want to miss out on that?

It's no wonder then that current brain research and consciousness studies verify what the ancient Christian monastic tradition has known all along by experience: that such daily practices as silence and stillness, attention and intention, literally change the brain's activity and reduce stress levels in the body, enabling higher level intuitive/creative thinking and deeper level feeling and perceptive knowing.

On a social level, the Unitive state is intimately linked with what we might refer to now as holiness, or the awareness that a person has deeply acquired a sanctity about them, what Jesus called "purity of heart." This sanctity may or may not manifest in unique and tangible ways, such as gifts of healing, discernment, counsel or teaching, to name a few.

Sanctity doesn't mean perfection either. It doesn't mean becoming less human, or becoming so "heavenly minded that you are no earthly good." Actually, it means just the opposite. It means that we grow more human, more real, more authentic, more free.

Paradoxically, beyond our self, we become ourselves. In Union with God, we become fierce love. For that reason, those who are given the grace of sanctity in the Unitive state are often, despite their chosen solitude, sought after for counsel, healing and spiritual guidance.

It's not that contemplation or the Unitive state are just for special people or saints either. Actually, they are for everyone, and available to all. Indeed, anyone who gives their life to God in response to God's call and grace; picks up a daily meditative prayer practice; listens for God's word in *lectio divina;* selflessly serves others, and regularly participates in worship and partakes in the Eucharist will often discover that they have become transformed, and have become more holy, as in a "wholeness" soaked with love and radiant with wisdom.

Those who live this way intentionally, will no doubt be brought into the contemplative/Unitive state in their experience with God and others – which is, at its core, a very beautiful way of seeing God, the self, the world and others. In my view, the world would benefit from more people living in and from this Unitive state.

In one sense, anyone in Christ already is in the Unitive state, but there is a difference between "accepting Jesus" and "following Christ," and being "conformed to the image" as a Son/Daughter. It's a difference of depth. A good description of the psycho-spiritual *experience* of the Unitive state that contemplation may lead one into is that "I don't know where I end and God begins."

It's not that I am God. Nor is it that God is me. It's a Union. The Union is not God. Nor is it me. It's quite literally – Christ. The union of my human nature and the divine nature. Christ is the technical, theological term that describes *that in me which is one with God.*

To be clear, it's not oneness, nor is it twoness. It's the mystery of spiritual Union. A participation (2 Peter 1.4).An example of this kind of Union, even if just for a fleeting moment, is our participation in the Eucharist.

Or, a further, albeit imperfect analogy of this Union, could be the self-transcending interconnectedness that we may fleetingly feel during love-making with a beloved – body and mind, soul and spirit.

Union is so fleeting because the moment we become aware of it, the experience of Union seems to slip away from our consciousness, since to be aware of it is to be separated into knower and known, subject and object; thus collapsing the Union into a sense of connected separateness. I aware of you. I aware of it, and *vice versa*.

There is nothing wrong or "less than" about our experiences of separate connectedness. These are very crucial and important experiences of being human. Jewish theologian Martin Buber famously termed them as an I-Thou relationship. Or what the church fathers called "perichoreses," which might be translated as "movement among and within relationally," which I take to be like a beautiful co-indwelling dance of being, sharing joy and love, one to the other. However, contemplatives and contemplative experiences are teaching us that our experience of Union is beyond this I-Thou relationality, this perichoresis. Some are even revealing that in and beyond Union, this relational dance seemingly disappears.

In Union, this I-Thou awareness may increasingly collapse from the inside by love and leaves in its place the experience of oneness. There is no longer just an I and a Thou. In Union, there is an Us of No One. Not One, Not Two. A Union. And that oneness, that Union, is Christ. As contemporary contemplative author Bernadette Roberts teaches, the Union is Christ and "Christ is a what, not a who."[13]

Whereas Jesus was born as the Christ, in the full and complete state of Union with God, we can be re-born into Christ, brought into the state of Union by grace. In, and then beyond Union, our Who-ness seemingly disappears from our awareness and is integrated into a What-ness. While some Who-ness is still there ontologically, increasing experiences in this state of Union may lead to an increasing transformation of one's Who-ness. Just as St.

Paul paradoxically said, "I, not I, Christ in me" (Galatians 2.20). This transformation may then birth a totally different way of being you, but also *not* you. It births a process of diminishment of one's self-essence or "me-dynamic" by the energy of the transformative Union.

A way Jesus invited us to follow and that St. Paul described as being "hidden with Christ in God" (Colossians 3.3). That there is something beyond our awareness and experience of Union is very important to welcome and explore. It's a path Bernadette Roberts calls the "path of no-Self." When there is no self, it means that all there is, is Union, and then beyond Union – what awaits us is the reality and mystery of literally being transformed into Christ. Beyond Union, there is no more self to know that it's in Union. *You simply are the Union and the Union is You.*

This kind of relational knowing is fearless because you begin to realize and experience that *literally* when you are in Christ nothing can separate you from the love of God. (cf. Romans 8.28-31). Increasingly you are no longer the same "you" in God. While God remains beyond your understanding and more than your conscious or unconscious experience and awareness, you at the same time are gratuitously becoming a participant in the divine nature (2 Peter 1.4), a living member of the body of Christ (1 Corinthians 12.27). Thus, the contemplative journey as well as the practice of Centering Prayer is a movement deeper in God through silence until, as St. Paul puts it, "Christ is all in all" (Colossians 3.11). That is to say, until there is only the mystery of the Union: "I, Not I, Christ in me." (Galatians 2.20). Beyond that who can say but very few, and Silence itself, which ever so wondrously, simply is *the* last word because it's also before all words.

Centering Prayer

So, moving from the larger picture of the contemplative spiritual journey, and the Unitive state, how does this relate with Centering Prayer? The short answer is that Centering Prayer is just one method of receptive prayer that can lead you to the fullness of contemplative prayer, and aid in the process of moving through the Dark Nights.

At its best, Centering Prayer is a receptive method of prayer that facilitates a deeper experience of abiding in Christ that can lead you to the interior state of contemplation, that is to say, simply being with God. This state of contemplation has been described by many as an inward way of seeing, as if the eye of God that sees you, is also the eye you see with.

Or, in other words, that place where God and you are one, a place where you can't tell where you end and God begins. That is the "place" the contemplative journey is moving us toward, and what the contemplative dimension of experience can cultivate in us.

In the same way there is a developmental path of ever deepening life in Christ, there is also a developmental path of prayer. Spiritually, we move more and more into realness and away from falseness, fear and all the unconscious appetites of the "flesh," which is a word that summarizes the mindset of living from self-me centeredness over against God. Such a profound movement will naturally effect your method of prayer.

So far, we've been taking a big picture look at the major milestones of the spiritual journey. As just mentioned, in a similar way that there is a developmental spiritual path with unique and identifiable milestones, there is also a developmental path of prayer. For many, the path of our prayer experience usually begins with requests to God for yourself and others. While perfectly appropriate and called for, there is certainly more to our prayer journey than asking God for things. If you are honest, you have probably experienced this recognition too, especially in the wake of moments where your prayers have not been answered, perhaps met by the void of silence.

In the void of silence, we are faced with the choice of resentment toward God or reframing the seeming silence as the answer we actually need but just cannot see why, at least at first. As we deepen in our faith and mature in our spiritual life, our prayer experience often moves from making requests to simply resting in God's presence.

I call this this movement "the spectrum of prayer." The spectrum of prayer moves from wordy prayers to silent prayers. On the one end, contemplative prayer.

On the other end, discursive (with words) prayer – one quite passive, the other quite active. One silent, the other vocal. Please know that it's not about one being better or more "spiritual" than the other. The Christian life should develop all channels on the prayer spectrum. The full

Christian life needs all of the forms of prayer on the band-width, just not all at once.

To put it differently: we rely upon different prayer methods at different stages on our spiritual journey and development, as well as in the different life events that we may be experiencing. As contemplative author Richard Rohr reminds us, "everything belongs," and there is a season for everything.

Unfortunately, too many Christians don't know about a whole segment of the prayer spectrum, and as a result they are missing out on the significant benefits that come from praying on the contemplative "wavelength."

To picture this prayer spectrum, here's a non-exhaustive sample that illustrates the movement from word based prayer to silent, receptive prayer. Please note there is no value judgment. Again, one is not better or more important than the other. Indeed, they are all interconnected, and depend upon the balancing of one to the other in our lives and in the church:

Discursive/Word based Prayers

    Liturgical Prayers

        Prayers of thanksgiving

            Intercessory Petitions

                Devotional Prayers of Surrender

                    The Jesus Prayer

                        Centering Prayer

                          Receptive/Contemplative Prayer

Many people, over the course of a dedicated prayer practice such as intercessory prayer or devotional prayer, begin to discover, quite naturally, that *after* they have "talked" with God or "asked from God," they begin to discover the joy of simply "resting with God." It's often a very natural process of growth in spiritual intimacy and trust, feeling increasing freedom to simply be with God versus talking to God. This happens to many people, and many people are actually having contemplative experiences without realizing it, or calling it that!

Just because the invitation is to a deeper form of prayer, please know that there is nothing wrong with vocal or liturgical prayers. Everything belongs and serves a vital purpose in our spiritual life. However, if you could grow deeper, wouldn't you want to know how?

By way of analogy, if you wished to experience another as a beloved not just as a friend, you wouldn't keep meeting in a public restaurant repeating a first date, talking to each other, trying to impress the other with your best self. You would, over a period of time, seek to move into the bedroom where you could experience, in wordless wonder, the full consummation and vulnerability of your love for each other. This may even involve a deeper level of authenticity and humiliation that may at first be quite uncomfortable. Real intimacy usually is – until the "me dynamic" is replaced by selfless love and surrender.

Thus, the spectrum of prayer identifies different, appropriate prayer practices that move from more exterior forms to more interior. From more wordy, to more silent. From discursive (with words) to contemplative (silent). From declarative to receptive.

We might describe receptive/contemplative prayer simply as *a resting or forgetting of oneself in God, without any awareness of separation or sense of twoness*. This experience of rest or self-forgetfulness may happen quite naturally and unexpectedly over the course of a Centering Prayer daily practice; almost imperceptibly, and often for very brief moments. It may come and it may go. For some, these moments might endure longer, perhaps even becoming a permanent state, which I mentioned earlier is traditionally referred to in the Christian tradition as the Unitive state.

Thus, if there were a simple tool that might foster and facilitate more of us moving into the Unitive state and seeing through the contemplative lens, would not I as a pastor and teacher wish to communicate the value of that tool and the importance of the method? And if there was such a practice that could heal what ails us and lead us into the fullness of what life was meant to be, conveying to each of us the fullness of joy in Christ, would you not also do everything you could to incorporate that practice into your life? Centering Prayer is just such a practice. It facilitates us into the contemplative experience of God, and from there, we can be drawn by grace, over time, into the complete joy of the Unitive state.

The more of us who partake in the daily graces of Centering Prayer; then the more of us will move deeper into the contemplative atmosphere and therefore be transformed into love. The more of us who will move into that contemplative atmosphere, the more of us will then become more complete saints in Christ, manifesting goodness, joy and justice in a world desperately in need of non-reactive, fearless, centered, peaceful people capable of loving their neighbor and forgiving their enemies quickly.

So, to summarize: Centering Prayer is a method of receptive prayer. The practice of Centering Prayer may lead one to the contemplative state of prayer, or more simply, that interior state of being and knowing and experiencing, often deeper than thought, where you are in God and God is in you. Practices such as Centering Prayer may lead to the interior experience of contemplative prayer, which is often an indication one is moving into the Unitive state.

Invitations:

Three reasons to practice Centering Prayer

Please practice Centering Prayer because Jesus invites you to meet Abba in the inner room of your heart (Matthew 6.6.)

Love is calling to you. God is love.

Named as Abba, this ever present depth of conscious love wishes for you to know it and feel it and become one with it.

The silence is the atmosphere in which this journey can come to its full completion.

If you are hungering for the fullness of life in God and for the life that Jesus demonstrated and invited us into, then by all means, delve into the silence with some form of meditative prayer.

Abba…an ancient word. That begins with the first sound emerging from the silence:

Ahhhhhhh….Welcome home.

Please practice Centering Prayer because the Trinity will graciously use it as a tool for your spiritual healing and transformation into love.

You will never be the same, and you will not regret it.

Parts of your self will resent it, but those parts are not your true self or your most utmost reality.

You are love.

And you were created for the consummation of love that happens after the howls and moans of everything else occurring in life. After the delights of the day and night, and after all the journeys one can take in a lifetime.

In the end, there is the sweet silence holding us as love, by love, for love, into love.

You'd want to know this. And would not want to miss out on the banquet.

Please practice Centering Prayer for the glory of God and the continued flourishing of our human civilization.

In the light of the modern discoveries of the unconsciousness, the expanding universe, the relationality of the quantum world, perhaps the Holy Spirit is calling us to new dimensions of prayer.

Dimensions intuited in every age by Christian mystics and insights that resonate with the ancient wisdom of the contemplative prayer practices.

Are we listening to the insights?

They are shedding new light on the gift of prayer and its extraordinary role in our present and future unfolding as a human species.

Benediction:

A prayer for your spiritual fruitfulness through Centering Prayer

God of Mercy:

You who are the first light in the depths of the deep, shine unexpected blessings upon our life outstretched to you.

Draw us into the silence to feel your closeness, and send us into the world with attentiveness to the movement of mercy in-between the extremes of All or Nothing. Through Christ our Lord we pray.

May God bless you in every way in the silence through Christ by the Spirit.

Amen.

Further Resources

Books

Carl Arico, *Taste of Silence: A Guide to the Fundamentals of Centering Prayer.*

Cynthia Bourgeault, *Centering Prayer and Inner Awakening,*

David Frenette, *The Path of Centering Prayer: Deepening Your Experience of God.*

Peter Traben Haas, *Centering Prayers: A One-Year Daily Companion for Going Deeper into the Love of God*

Thomas Keating, *Open Mind, Open Heart*

Basil Pennington, *Centered Living: The Way of Centering Prayer.*

Web

ContemplativeChristians.com

ContemplativeOutreach.org

ConsciousHarmony.org

Contemplation.com

About the Author

Dr. Peter Traben Haas serves as a Teaching Pastor in the Presbyterian Church (USA). Peter earned his M.Div. from Princeton Seminary and a Doctorate of Ministry from Austin Presbyterian Theological Seminary. Peter is a certified Centering Prayer instructor and retreat leader, and is the author of multiple books and articles on the contemplative Christian dimension, and founder of ContemplativeChristians.com.

Endnotes

[1] Kierran Kavanaugh and Otilio Rodriguez, Trans., *The Collected Works of St. John of the Cross* (Washington, D.C, ICS Publications, 1979) 116.

[2] Ibid., 117.

[3] Thomas Merton, *New Seeds of Contemplation* (Boston: MA, Shambhala, 2003) 42-43.

[4] For an exceptional discussion of John Calvin's view of the mystical union, see Dennis E. Tamburello, *Union with Christ: John Calvin and the Mysticism of St. Bernard* (Louisville, KY: Westminster/John Knox, 1994).

[5] John Calvin, *Institutes of the Christian Religion,* edited by John T. McNeill, trans. Ford Lewis Battles, 3.11.10 (Philadelphia: The Westminster Press, 1960).

[6] Karl Barth, *Church Dogmatics,* II/2: *The Doctrine of God.* Edited b G.W. Bromiley and T.F. Torrance. Translated by T.H.L. Parker et al. (Edinburgh, T & T Clark, 1957) 30.

[7] Thomas Keating, *Open Mind, Open Heart,* (New York, Continuum, 2007) 2.

[8] Adam Neder, *Participation in Christ: An Entry into Karl Barth's Church Dogmatics* (Louisville, KY: Westminster John Knox Press, 2009) 20.

[9] Frances Kelly Nemeck and Marie Theresa Coombs, *Contemplation* (Eugene: Oregon, Wifp and Stock Publishers, 2001) 116.

[10] Michael Washburn, *The Ego and the Dynamic Ground: A*

Transpersonal Theory of Human Development (Albany: NY, The State University Press of New York, 1988) 141-142.

[11] Ibid.

[12] Andrew Louth, "Theology, Contemplation and the University" in *Studia Theologica,* I, 2/2003, 66-67. See also. *The Origins of the Christian Mystical Tradition: From Plato to Denys* (Oxford: Oxford University Press, 2007).

[13] Bernadette Roberts, *What Is Self?: A Study of the Spiritual Journey in Terms of Consciousness* (Boulder, CO: Sentient Publications, 2004).

Made in the USA
San Bernardino, CA
22 October 2016